UN

THE PROPHETIC

IN US

You too can prophesy

My sheep listen to My voice, and I know them, and they follow Me.
John 10:27

By Fay Velez

Copyright © 2024 by Nita Fay Velez

This book is dedicated to all the people that are trying to hear the voice of God and obey what He is saying. The keys in this book are to enlighten people about how easy it is to unlock the prophetic gifts inside of us.

Published 2024

TABLE OF CONTENTS

Table of Contents

Fay Velez

INTRODUCTION

I am writing this from the viewpoint of knowing how easy it is to hear the voice of God. God is wanting us to all get out of our comfort zone and allow Him to stretch us and to use us in our prophetic gifting. The purpose of this book is to give you several stories of how I trusted God and did what He told me to do, and the amazing breakthroughs I saw in doing this. God wants us to know that we hear His voice, and He does not want us to doubt that. He wants us to step out with boldness and confidence in knowing that we hear Him clearly. My prayer is when you read this book that you will find, just as I did, that God wants us to talk to Him and He wants to talk to us. We just have to trust that and step out and allow Him to use us.

This book will give you different ways we can hear the voice of God. It will tell you what to do and how to stretch that way of hearing God's voice in your own life.

It will teach you how prophets receive revelation and direction from the Lord for our benefit, and how they can see into the future and tell us things that will keep us from making wrong decisions. Or, to warn us about something that is coming.

My prayer is that you will learn from this book to unlock the prophetic in you, not only to hear for yourself but for others as well.

About the Author:

Fay Velez is an ordained Christian International (CI) Minister. Her and her husband Tom lead the Prophetic Healing and Deliverance Ministry at Vision Church at the Christian International Headquarters (VCCI) in Santa Rosa Beach, Florida. They also lead the 8:30am daily morning prayer meeting Monday – Friday, and the 7pm VCCI communion service, live on Monday nights.

They are also on the Prophetic team and have a traveling ministry.

Fay is on staff at Christian International as the Director of the Vision Investment Partner program.

Fay holds a Biblical degree from CI, and functions in the fivefold ministry office of a Prophet. She is especially gifted in the discerning of spirits, deliverance, prophecy, prophetic counseling, spiritual warfare, healing, and intercession.

Fay and her husband Tom have been teaching and ministering on prayer, the gifts of the Holy Spirit, prophesying over individuals, doing personal deliverance, and administering the Lord's healing through the wonderful name of Jesus Christ for over 35 years.

They have both led many to Jesus and have led many into the Baptism of the Holy Spirit with the evidence of speaking in tongues.

CHAPTER 1 Tongues and an intimate relationship with the Lord

The purpose of reading and understanding this book is so you can just step out and prophecy over someone and not be afraid of messing up. When we first start out prophesying, do not say anything mean or hurtful. Do not tell them who they are supposed to marry or to sell their house or give you money. You are not to prophesy for your own benefit, but for the benefit of the person you are prophesying to. We are only supposed to encourage, build up and edify each other.

As you read this book, raise your expectations to a greater level. Expect to grow and mature in the Lord. Expect to hear the voice of God and do not doubt it.

One of the main ways we can really connect with God and hear His voice clearly is to purpose in our heart to die to ourselves. This means to set aside our own personal ambitions and desires. Allow God to purify us and always remember, we will be held accountable. Strive to walk a strong walk with the Lord. Do not compromise in what you believe. Do not doubt but stand firm and do not be moved.

I really believe for us to be able to prophecy the way the Lord desires us to, is that we need to speak in tongues.

There is power in our prayer language, and when we pray in tongues the enemy cannot understand what we are saying, so he cannot interfere. When we pray in tongues, we are praying exactly what needs to be prayed.

I say that our tongues are a hotline to the Lord. Nothing can stop or hinder our prayers we are praying in tongues.

Do not be afraid to receive the baptism of the Holy Spirit with the evidence of speaking in tongues. God's word in Matthew 7:9-11 says which of you, if your son asks for bread, will give him a stone? Or if he asks for a fish, will give him a snake? If you, then, though your evil, know how to give good gifts to your children, how much more will your Father in heaven give good gifts to those who ask him?

What this verse says is that no loving father would give a stone or a snake to his hungry son if he asked for a piece of bread or fish. Jesus is saying the same thing: that his heavenly Father will give his children good gifts a well.

Below are some scriptures about speaking in tongues when you are filled with the Holy Spirit:

Acts 2:4 And they were all filled with the Holy Spirit and began to speak with other tongues, as the Spirit gave them utterance.

Acts 8:16-18 For as yet He had fallen upon none of them. They had only been baptized in the name of the Lord Jesus. Then they laid hands on them, and they received the Holy Spirit. And when Simon saw that through the laying on of the apostles' hands the Holy Spirit was given, he offered them money,

Acts 10:44-48 While Peter was still speaking these words, the Holy Spirit fell

on all who were listening to the message.
And the believers from among the
circumcised <the Jews> who came with
Peter were surprised [and] amazed,
because the free gift of the Holy Spirit had
been bestowed [and] poured out largely
even on the Gentiles. For they heard them
talking in <unknown> tongues (languages)
and extolling [and] magnifying God. Then
Peter asked, can anyone forbid [or] refuse
water for baptizing these people, seeing
that they have received the Holy Spirit just
as we have? And he ordered that they be
baptized in the name of Jesus Christ (the
Messiah). Then they begged him to stay
on there for some days.

Acts 19:2-6 And he asked them; did you
receive the Holy Spirit when you believed
<on Jesus as the Christ>? And they said,
no, we have not even heard that there is a
Holy Spirit. And he asked, into what
<baptism> then were you baptized? They
said, Into John's baptism. And Paul said,
John baptized with the baptism of
repentance, continually telling the people
that they should believe in the One Who
was to come after him, that is, in Jesus
<having a conviction full of joyful trust

that He is Christ, the Messiah, and being obedient to Him>. On hearing this they were baptized <again, this time> in the name of the Lord Jesus. And as Paul laid his hands upon them, the Holy Spirit came on them; and they spoke in <foreign, unknown> tongues (languages) and prophesied.

Also, consider: Acts 10:38 (Jesus moved in power AFTER He got the baptism of Holy Spirit after John the Baptist prayed & baptized Jesus)

Acts 10:38 How God anointed Jesus of Nazareth with the Holy Spirit and with power, who went about doing good and healing all who were oppressed by the devil, for God was with Him.

Luke 11:9-13 (you will get the right spirit) So I say to you, ask, and it will be given to you; seek, and you will find; knock, and it will be opened to you. For everyone who asks receives, and he who seeks finds, and to him who knocks it will be opened. If a son asks for bread from any father among you, will he give him a stone? Or if [he asks] for a fish, will he give him a serpent instead of a fish? Or if he asks for an egg, will he offer him a scorpion? If you then, being evil, know how to give good gifts to your children, how much more will [your] heavenly Father give the Holy Spirit to those who ask Him.

If you want to receive the baptism of the Holy Spirit with the evidence of speaking in tongues. Just pray this prayer out loud.

Prayer: (Pray this prayer out loud)

Lord, I ask you to forgive me of my sins in Jesus' name. Lord, I ask You to baptism me in the Holy Spirit with the evidence of speaking in tongues in Jesus' name. Lord, I believe that when I ask, I will receive and that when I open my mouth, I will speak in tongues in Jesus' name. Amen

God is a personal God and He is a jealous God. He wants an intimate relationship with us. We cannot allow sin to be in our lives. Sin will dull our communication with God. We will not be able to hear His voice. None of us are perfect, we all mess up and we all make mistakes.

If you have sin in your life, you will not feel God close to you. The Holy Spirit does not share a temple with sin.

1 Corinthians 6:19 tells us we are the temple of the Holy Ghost. God wants His temple to be pure and holy. When we mess up and we repent God's closeness returns. So do not be hard on yourself. It is God's desire that we stay connected with Him. I am a firm believer that as long as we do not stop trying, we have not failed. The only way we fail is if we quit.

Sin will block our relationship with the Lord, and it will block us from hearing His voice. As you are reading this book if there is any sin in your life get rid of it. We do not want anything to hinder us from receiving all God has for us or keeping us from hearing His voice clearly.

As you are reading this book take a minute or two and check your heart. Make sure you are pure before the Lord.

Fay Velez

CHAPTER 2 What do we do with our prophetic words

When you receive a prophetic word, whether you heard it directly from God or through someone else, write it down. Take it to someone you trust and let them read it, and help you understand it. Do not take a recorded word to your leader, overseer, or Pastor for them to listen to and help you understand it. Take time to write it down, so they have it written down before them.

I go to Vision Church Christian International in Santa Rosa Beach, Fl. They teach you to always write your prophetic words down. I go places all the time and I hear people say, oh yes, I have my prophetic word recorded and I listen to it all the time. I believe, most of the time, until you write it down, you will not get the whole meaning of the word.

When a prophet speaks, a lot of times they do not take time to pause after each sentence, they are just flowing with the Holy Spirit. When you write it down, it will make so much more sense to you.

I know myself when I speak, I speak very fast. A lot of times I do not stop until I am finished. If you do not write your prophetic word down, you will only remember bits and pieces of the word. Most of the time you remember it the way you want it to be.

When you write your words down, it comes alive. Even the periods and commas being in the right places makes the word read different. So, write your words down and war with them. Take your word and write out decrees and decree them out loud daily.

I have around 170 decrees that I decree every day. I take my prophetic words and I write them out and make decrees out of them. An example of how I make them into decrees is:

The prophet said, there is a multiplication anointing coming to me and my husband. He said doors were opening for us to go to churches and help develop ministry teams. He said doors were opening for us to go to the continent God has called us to, and that it would spread to the north, south, east, and west.

There was a lot more in the prophetic words we have received. But this is enough to show you how to take your prophetic word and write it into a decree. Be sure you say your decrees out loud.

I decree that the multiplication anointing that was prophesied over us to come forth in Jesus' name. I decree doors to open for us to go to churches and help develop ministry teams in Jesus' name. I decree doors to open for us to go to the continent God has called us to in Jesus' name, and that it would spread to the north, south, east, and west in Jesus' name.

It is so important to revisit your prophetic words and put into action whatever you need to do to make these words come to pass in your life. But remember that God's timing is not our timing and if He says this will happen soon it could be several years down the road. We have to always do what our hands find us to do while we are waiting for our prophetic words to be fulfilled.

Do not get a word and just sit on that word and do nothing. God 's word says that a righteous man's steps are ordered by the Lord, so we have to start stepping (moving). I believe we have to give God something to work with. When we are just sitting and saying we are just waiting on God. He is saying I am waiting on you. So get involved with your church and be a part. No matter what we are doing, it is still ministry.

CHAPTER 3 What does prophecy do

Prophecy helps us equip and train others. We need to know God's word, so we can weigh the prophetic words we received by the word of God. If the word you received does not agree with the word of God, throw it away. Our prophetic word should always line up with God's word.

We can all hear the voice of God. God's word says my sheep hears my voice, and I know them, and they follow me.
John 10:27

It does not matter about our age. We all can hear and feel the touch and voice of the Lord. So many times, my husband and I have lost things, and we would pray and ask God where it was, and God would tell us. God loves to talk to us and to spend time with us.

One time my husband Tom lost his keys, and we could not find them. We looked everywhere. I was in the garage looking and I said God show me where those keys are at. He said go look in the laundry basket. I went and looked and there they were.

Another time we put our smaller suitcases into our larger ones trying to make some room. About 1 month later we had a ministry trip we were going on. We looked everywhere for our small suitcases, and we could not find them. I ask God where those suitcases were at. He said go look in the larger suitcases. I did and there they were.

My husband Tom and I head up the morning prayer a Vision Church Christian International Monday – Friday each week. During our prayer time one morning God just begin to download to me that He was giving me a house. We were not asking God for a house. It was just the two of us. Our children are all grown up. So, we had bought a mobile home and put it on campus at Vision Church Christian International where many of the staff lived at the time.

We were very content with our mobile home. We were really not there that much.

It was paid for, so we were good. But that morning in prayer God just begin to tell me He was giving us a house. He told me where to go, who to talk to about buying our mobile home. It was in detail. God had it all laid out for us. After prayer I told my husband what God had said. I begin to tell him everything God said. God had said for us to head toward where my hairdresser's shop was at the time. We took that as we were supposed to go to Freeport in Florida. When we went there, we did not feel any peace. So, we headed back.

We are at the church at least twelve times each week. We knew we had to be close to the church. As we were heading back, God said turn into Peach Creek Subdivision. So, we did! Peach Creek Subdivision is only about 3 minutes from the church.

They were just starting phase 5 housing development. I told my husband Tom this is it. Let's stop by the office and talk to them. We had a ministry trip planned to go to South Korea the next day. My husband said let's just wait until we return from South Korea. I said I really feel we need to stop now. So, we did. We did not know it at the time, but there was a long list of people waiting for these lots.

We told the lady at the Peach Creek office that we really wanted the lot where they were planning to put a four bedroom and three car garage home. She said we will let you know. My husband, some of our friends and I began to call in that lot. We left for our 2-week trip to South Korea. The lady in the office told us to check back with her when we returned. While we were in South Korea, the lady in the office sent us an email saying we got the lot. That in itself was supernatural.

What was so awesome was we were able to tell them what we wanted in our home since they had not started the house yet. If we had waited and talked to them after we returned from South Korea that lot would have been gone. We love our house, and we are so glad when God spoke to me that neither of us questioned it, we just moved on it.

God knew what He was doing, and we did not have a clue. Right after we sold our mobile home and moved into our new home, Vision Church Christian International gave all the people that were living in the mobile homes on campus notice that they would be selling the property. Everyone had to be out within 6 months.

Since we had already sold our mobile home before we knew about that portion of the campus property being sold, we got top dollar for our mobile home because we did not have to rush to sale it.

God blessed us in an amazing way. We are so glad we did not question what God had said to us. It is so awesome to ask, listen, and hear the voice of God. But it is double awesome when you do not even ask, and He speaks so clearly to you.

We can all hear the voice of God; we just have to listen. So many times, when we say we cannot hear anything, it is because we are trying too hard. It is so important to relax and just have fun. I am a firm

believer that if we open our mouth God
will fill it with His words. We just have to
trust Him and not doubt.

CHAPTER 4 God communicates with us

God wants to communicate with us. He wants us to hear His voice. He wants us to know His voice. It is His desire to communicate His desires, plans, and purposes to us. We have to get out of the way and let God fill us with His desires, instead of us being focused on our own selfish desires. God always knows what is best for us. We have to trust Him even when we do not know what is going on. Communicating is a vital part of God's personality. He is the living word, and He loves to talk and communicate with us.

Bible history demonstrates that God communicated. He communicated to man and to all creation. He spoke to Adam and Eve. He spoke to the serpent. He spoke to Cain and many other people in the Bible.

I want to tell you a couple of stories about how I heard the voice of God. I was in college, and I would study and go to college and God would supernaturally help me remember the answers to the questions on the tests. God always says if we do our part, He will do His part. One day I went to college, and I knew I had a test, but I had not studied. So, I sat down to take the test and I was waiting on God and He was no where to be found. I was calling Him saying God where are you. Needless to say, I got a sixty on that test. I was so upset and mad. I got in my car, and I said GOD where were you. He said I was there, but if you do not study, I cannot help you. You have to do your part and then I will always do my part. I learned a lesson that night. You better believe from that day forward I was prepared, and God never let me down.

God speaks to us as well and He loves to talk to us. We have to believe that He speaks and that we can hear Him.

Even though God speaks, and He wants us to hear his voice, our actions can communicate to others without us saying anything. Have you ever tried to talk to someone, and they just rolled their eyes? Even though they did not say anything you still understood what their feelings were. I used to work at a after school program and one Mother's Day the boss's daughter gave me a Mother's Day card. When she gave me the card, I thought how sweet. After I read the card, it really shook me. The card said how sweet and kind I was and that she had never seen anyone that lived a Godly life like I did. I was like oh wow what if I had had a bad day. I would have destroyed my testimony to that young girl, and I did not even know she was watching me. We need to always be aware of others around us. We never know who is watching us. I never said anything to that young girl. She saw who I was by my actions not by my words.

Prophecy is not just for others. Hearing God's voice is for us as well. Hearing God's voice gives us courage to arise above our circumstances, to go forward when we are discouraged.

His voice brings purpose and unity to us. It helps us fulfill the destiny God has for us. His voice reveals strategies and directions to us. We hear God's voice through His written word, through the Holy Spirit and through His prophets.

One church service my husband Tom and I were at when we lived in Alabama, the pastor stopped the service. He looked at me and He said: "God said to tell you that Tom would live and not die". Tom and I did not think much about it, because we thought he was fine. About 3 months later we found out that Tom had esophagus cancer. The doctor did not give him much chance. But I grabbed hold of that prophetic word, and I began to war with it. God did a miracle in my husband and he is a living testimony of it today.

Another time God used a prophet to tell me something about a job I was really wanting. At the time I worked at a plant and there was a warehouse job that came open. I just knew I was getting that job. I had prayed and asked God to give it to me, but I did not get it. I was devastated and I really was confused and did not understand why I did not get it. About 3 weeks later a prophet came to our church and he prophesied over me. He told me the reason I did not get that job was that God had something so much better for me. A few weeks later I got a weight counselor job, and I loved it. Again, we have to trust God that He knows best even when we cannot see Him working.

God uses prophets to bring peace, hope and encouragement to us and to others. God made our ears to hear. Hearing God's voice should be easy. He desires to talk to us, and we need to desire to prophecy.

Fay Velez

CHAPTER 5 Word of knowledge

Prophecy sometimes comes in a word of knowledge. The word of knowledge is one of the gifts of the Holy Spirit. A word of knowledge is an instant knowledge from the Lord that the person has no way of knowing unless God reveals it. The word of knowledge goes straight to the heart, and it opens a door for God to minister.

A word of knowledge could be that someone has back pain, shoulder pain or knee pain.

Several years ago, I was at Vision Church Christian International, and I was in their Ministering Spiritual Gifts training, known now as Prophetic Training.

The instructor asked us all to ask God for a word of knowledge. We all had to line up across the front. People were saying things like back pain, stomach issues and headaches. God told me someone has a hole in their heart, and it had been there since birth.

The other words of knowledge that people were getting were all good.

But most of the time if you have a group of people and someone calls out headaches, back pain, or stomach issues. someone in the group will have that. Since my word was so specific and rare, I knew that I was either hearing God or I was missing Him. I stepped out and said what God had given me. It seem like an hour went by and nobody said anything.
It was really just a few minutes, but it seemed much longer.

Finally, a man in the back of the room said I have a hole in my heart, and it has been there since birth. I was able to pray for him, and I was so excited that God used me. We should never be afraid to step out.

Another time I was doing this activation, and God told me someone had an infected big toe. Again, either I heard God, or I did not. I stepped out and gave what God give me. This man said it is me, my toe has been infected for a long time. He said it will not get well. I got to pray for him, and again I was so excited how God used me. Just the other day one of my best friends was at my house. She had cut the end of her finger very badly a few days before. While we were spending time together, God told me to pray for her finger. She had a band aid on it, so I just took her hand and prayed. She called me the next day she said she was taking a shower, and she could not get her finger wet because it would bleed. The band aid got wet anyway, she said when she took the band aid off, the nail had grown back, and it was no longer bleeding. God did a miracle in her finger. We have to be ready and willing to step out when God tells us to step out.

My husband Tom and I were at the skin doctor. The doctor came in and she said I am sorry I am late, but my back is really hurting. After she finished checking my husband, I asked her if I could pray for her. She allowed me to pray for her and the pain immediately left. Again, we have to be willing to allow the Lord to use us.

I know I have told several stories, but I tell these stories to build your faith. A word of knowledge is not a long sentence or a paragraph. It is one to three words. Example back pain, headache, or knee pain etc.

CHAPTER 6 Discerning of spirits

The discerning of spirits is a great tool to have when you are prophesying. It lets you see into, or sense, the darkness and what is going on in the spirit realm. This can even allow you to see the motive of people's hearts.

Being able to decern just one word for someone could change that person's life forever.

There was a pastor, I wish I could remember his name. He tells a story about this young man that came into his service. Before he came into the service this young man told God if you are real, when I go into this church let the pastor tell me that Jesus loves me. The young man told God if this pastor does not tell me this, I am going to kill myself.

The young man came into the church service. The pastor did not know him. He came in and sat down. In the middle of the pastor's sermon. The pastor looked over at him and he said son I do not know you, but God told me to tell you "Jesus loves you." The young man begin to cry. He told the pastor what he had told God. The young man got saved that day. Just that one sentence was so powerful that it changed a young man's life.

We need to allow God's anointing to rise-up within us to speak forth His word. With boldness and confidence.

Another pastor tells a story I do not remember his name either. But in the middle of his service, he started doing push-ups. This young guy said he had told God, God if you are real have the pastor do push-ups. This young man got saved as well. We have to have our ears tuned to the Lord and open our heart to Him, to be one He can flow though. The Lord is looking for vessels that He can flow through. Let's be that vessel.

My husband Tom and I head up the deliverance ministry at Vision Church Christian International in Santa Rosa Beach, Fl. We have seen the importance of having the gift of discernment. When we do deliverance on people, these people will say to us: how did you know that about me? Nobody knew that about me.

When we tell them that we just listen to the Holy Spirit, they are amazed. They are shocked at the freedom they receive. It is always fun when someone comes for deliverance that has only been saved for a short period of time. They have no clue what to expect. God always shows up and shows off. I believe He does this so they can see and know how big and real He is.

My husband Tom and I travel and minister. We were at this one church. We were headed up to the pulpit to preach. The pastor got up before us, and she said I want everyone to know that I have not told this couple anything about anyone in this church. We had done our "Get Free Stay Free" training for her church that weekend and we were doing the Sunday morning service as well. She said people kept coming up to her afterward, and asking why did you tell them that about me. So, it was awesome knowing we heard the voice of God so clearly. It really builds our faith when we get feedback. But even when we do not, we know God speaks and we know we hear Him.

Another time we went to this Christian concert of a well-known speaker. When we walked in the sanctuary, I told my husband something was not right about that person. Later we found out that soon after that, he got a divorce and had been doing a lot of things that were not pleasing to the Lord.

Another time we went to this church where a well-known speaker was speaking and who was highly respected. When we pulled into the parking lot, I told my husband something was not right. Later we found out that the pastor of the church was messing with the children in the church, and soon thereafter wound up being arrested, convicted, and went to prison.

Having a gift of discernment is an amazing tool to have. I walk strongly in the gift of discernment. When I first found out that I had this gift, I would seem to always see the bad things in people's lives. We could be at a gathering, and everyone would be having a great time in the room laughing and enjoying the fellowship. When I walked in the room God started showing me things that were in people's heart and the motives of people. I told my husband: I do not want this gift. I seem to just always see the negative things. He said Fay don't you dare quench that gift. We will all have to have that gift in the end times. So, embrace it. As I grew in the Lord, I was able to handle it better. Now I thank God for giving me that gift, especially since we do deliverance all the time. Since I walk in such a strong gift of discernment, I am going to put a prayer below for you to pray over yourselves to receive a greater gift of discernment.

Prayer:
Lord, I ask You to give me a greater gift of discernment, in Jesus' name. Lord, let me be one that will walk in a room and know the true motive of people's hearts, in Jesus' name. Lord, let me be able to discern the plans and strategies of the enemy, so I can come against them before

they come against me and turn it back on them, in Jesus' name. Lord, help me be able to discern wolves in sheep clothing that come into the church to try and bring strive and division to the church, in Jesus' name. Lord, grant me discernment against the deception of deceiving spirits, those spirits that claim Your name but do not know or seek Your heart in Jesus' name. Lord, I ask You to give me both discernment and wisdom. Lord, let me walk in Your supernatural revelation and knowledge in all I do, in Jesus' name. Thank You Lord, that from this day forward I will walk in discernment in a level I have not walked in before, in Jesus' name. Amen

CHAPTER 7 Prophetic praise

Prophetic praise is one of the greatest weapons of spiritual warfare. Praise is an offensive weapon designed by God against his enemies. Our praise is a demonstration or an expression that brings revenge on the enemy.

Worship brings release. When we worship God in spirit and in truth, it releases an atmosphere of alignment with us and the Lord in the spirit, and with others. It opens doors for us to hear the voice of God.

We need to expect that when we are in that type of atmosphere, we can do things we could not do before. We have to allow God to stretch us. We have to get out of our comfort zone. If we allow the presence of God, it will stir within us.

It puts us in the right attitude to receive, communicate with the Lord and to hear the voice of God. When we are in the atmosphere of praise, we see miracles and healings occur in our lives. When we do not feel well, and we start praising and worshiping the Lord things will shift for us.

My husband and I were in South Korea ministering. We were scheduled to minister in about an hour. All of a sudden, I just did not feel well. I turned on my praise music and began to worship and praise the Lord. After about 30 minutes I felt fine and was able to minister.

Praise is truly a weapon of war. It can always be used to stop the enemy or to shift our situations.

Worship and praise also opens the door for us to prophecy by song. Prophecy by song is when we have a spontaneous prophetic song of prophecy, praise, love, adoration, healing, deliverance, and warfare. It flows out of someone by song.

A prophetic song brings healing and deliverance when it is released. Many times, the worship leader will begin to sing a prophetic song or a song of the Lord. While he or she is singing people will be healed, set free and delivered. It is a powerful time when that happens.

Fay Velez

CHAPTER 8 Nabi prophet

A Nabi prophet can be defined as one who speaks or sings by the inspiration of God. This is a prophet where the words bubble up and they come out, and flow out in words, sentences, or phrases bubbling up from within the prophet who is giving the word.

I am mainly a Nabi prophet. When I open my mouth and prophecy, the words flow out like a river. Most of the time when someone stands in front of me, I do not have anything, but the minute I open my mouth the Lord fills it, and it just flows.

I was doing a ladies' conference and God told me to prophecy over everyone at the conference. Now I had prophesied a lot, but I had never prophesied over a whole church before. He said after you finish your message start on the front row and go down the row. He said prophesy one by one until you have finished every row. To be honest I was a little intimidated, but I stepped out and God filled my mouth.

Ever since that day I have never been afraid to prophecy.

If it is two people or three hundred, I am fine with it. I know that when I open my mouth God will fill it.

The first time my husband and I went to South Korea we had to prophecy over hundreds of people and each one we did it had to be interpreted. We were in this room and the line of the people to be prophesied over seemed like it went on forever. Time and time again God has been with my husband and me. I know He will always fill my mouth.

Another church we went to had 350 to 400 people and at the end of the service my husband and I had to prophesy over all of them, plus it all had to be interpreted. They would make two lines counting off 1, 2, 1, 2. My husband would take the ones and I would take the twos. It was an amazing time, but it also stretched us. God was always faithful, and he never let our mouths run dry.

When you prophecy over someone do not get upset if you feel like you have missed it. When my husband and I first started prophesying, I would say to him when we finished, I did not feel anything, I hope I did not miss it. It would never fail every time I did that, I would get a phone call, someone would come up to me or I would get a text, and people would say something like: wow the word you gave me was so right on, and it blessed me so much.

We cannot go on feelings. We have to just step out and open our mouth and believe God to fill it.

A seer prophet can also receive the word of the Lord the same way as a nabi prophet does, and vice versa. Again, we cannot put God in a box.

Amos 3:7-8 says, surely the Lord God does nothing, unless He reveals His secret to His servants the prophets.

Fay Velez

CHAPTER 9 The importance of our prophetic words

Prophetic words are awesome to use as a tool to war with. I love it when I am going through a situation or circumstance, and I do not understand what is going on and God will bring back one of my prophetic words to my mind. I will go get it and take that word and go to war with it. Again, this is why it is so important to write your prophetic words down. Put them in a notebook or in a file on your computer. Have them at your fingertips at all times.

A good example of me using me and my husband's prophetic words as a tool to war was when we found out Tom had esophagus cancer and the doctors gave him only a 5 percent chance of surviving the cancer, and only a 45 percent chance of even making it through the surgery.

I went to our prophetic words, and I found the words that prophets had prophesied over us that said my husband Tom would live a long healthy life. Tom even had one prophetic word that said he would live so long that he would start saying God it is time.

I took those words, and I began to go to war with them, decreeing that he would live and not die, that he would live a long healthy life, that we would fulfill all the promises that God had given us, in Jesus' name.

You can wage war with your prophetic words and come against the lies Satan is telling you. Remind him of what God has said to you through a prophetic word. Remind him of his future.

Speak your prophetic words over the circumstance that you are facing. As you do, watch them turn around for your good and for the glory of God.

CHAPTER 10 Prophetic ministry

Prophetic ministry is exciting because it is God communicating to us in the now: in the present. It is exciting because it gives us the opportunity of knowing and seeing into the heart and mind of God.

I believe being a strong intercessor opens the doors for us to hear the voice of God so much easier. Being a prayer warrior is a great benefit to hearing the voice of God. Having a close communion with the Lord opens the door as well.

Prophecy is one of the manifestations or gifts of the spirit. Prophecy is just speaking edification, exhortation, or comfort to people.

There are three levels of the operation of the prophetic in the church.
1. The occasional manifestation of the gift of prophecy (1 Cor chapter 12)
2. A consistent operation of the gift of prophecy (1 Cor chapter 12)
3. The fivefold ministry office of a prophet (Eph 4:11)

Eph 4:11 And He Himself gave some to be apostles, some prophets, some evangelists, and some pastors and teachers

All three function and operate under the manifestation of the same Holy Spirit.

The occasional or even the consistent gift of prophecy is available to all believers, and we should all desire it. These bring words of edification, exhortation, and comfort.

The fivefold ministry gift of the office of a prophet is a higher level of prophecy. Not all Christians are called and authorized by the Lord to flow at this level of authority and responsibility. This level has a greater authority to bring words of direction, correction, instruction, and motivation. It is often accompanied by an impartation of anointing and gifts.

God uses prophecy to transfer His words to the people. God calls His prophets spokespersons. It is God's purpose to tell the thoughts and intents of His heart to His prophets. God reveals His secrets to His servants the prophets, things that are not revealed to others.

A prophet is God's mouthpiece, God's spokesperson to the people. A prophet speaks the words that God puts in their mouth. They may speak a prophetic word by prophetic prayer, prophetic song, or prophetic actions.

An example of how this works is the prophetic flow could have a spoken word, and part of it comes in a song, another part in a prayer and maybe another part in a dance. While this is being done people are being healed, set free and touched by the power of God.

They can be used separately as well. That prophet doing the ministry can be a nabi (hearer) prophet, a seer prophet, or a sensor prophet.

The difference between a nabi, seer and senor are like I said earlier a nabi flows words like a river. A seer normally sees pictures or visions and they explain what they are seeing. A sensor senses something it could be good, or it could be bad. They just sense what is going on, and speak it forth.

We do not need to put God in a box. Whether we are a nabi prophet, a seer, or a sensor, we all hear the voice of God and we should speak it forth no matter which way we receive it.

It can come into our spirit without sound, where the only person who hears it is the person God is speaking it to.

We may also hear God in an audible voice. God's audible voice is as real and clear as if someone in the room with you was speaking. This is usually a very rare event.

A good example of this is in 1 Samuel 3:2-9 when Samual heard God's voice while he was serving under Eli in the temple as a young boy.

I have only heard the audible voice of God one time. It scared me half to death. I know many people talk about hearing God's voice audible and how awesome it was. When I heard His voice, it was a rebuke. I was not a Christian, and this was before I married my husband now. I was doing things I knew I was not supposed to be doing. I had plans to meet someone after work. God spoke to me, and He said if you go and meet this person you will not make it home alive. It scared me so bad that I had to leave work. I was trembling. I did not go meet that person and that ordeal changed my life.

I know without a doubt if I had disobeyed God and went after He told me not to, I would have died on my way home and I would be in hell today. It makes me shake even now to even think about the what ifs.

We can hear God or sense God by having a thought in our mind, an impression, a vison, or a dream. God can also use natural events to communicate His message to us.

In Jeremiah 18:1-10 God spoke to Jeremiah at the potter's house. Jeremiah

heard God's words as God used the
natural process of a potter working at his
wheel to convey His plan for a nation.

Know that prophetic words for individuals
are most of the time conditional. Many
people get a prophetic word, and they say
well that prophet missed it, that never
happened in my life. We have to put
action to our prophetic words: to cooperate
with the prophecy.

For example, if you get a prophetic word
that says you will be a doctor. If you do
not go to medical school, you will not be a
doctor. The prophet did not miss it. That
was God's plan for you, but you did not do
your part.

In the same way if a prophet tells us we
will walk in divine health, but we do not
put into our bodies what is good for us and
all we eat is junk food, we cannot expect
to have divine health.

We have four children. When our
youngest one was born, a prophet
prophesied over her that she would always

walk in divine health. It is amazing how this word is and has come to pass in her life. She would never eat processed foods growing up. She always ate fruits and vegetables. Our other three children loved fast food. She would not eat it. I do not think she even ate french fries until she was in middle school.

When our children were small my husband traveled a lot for work. I homeschooled so we went on a lot of his work trips with him. We would have to stop places to eat where she could get salads, vegetables, and fruit. She is over 30 years old now and she has two boys. She still eats healthily and exercises every day. Her two boys were raised to eat healthily as well. It is normal to see them walk around with a bag of baby carrots eating on them.

She is in amazing health. She does her apart and when we do our part God will do His part.

Fay Velez

CHAPTER 11 Warring over your prophetic words.

We have to war with our prophetic words. When we get a prophetic word, the devil hears it too. He comes immediately to steal it from us. God's word tells us in John 10:10 that the thief comes to steal and kill and destroy. That is why it is so important to write your prophetic words down. If you have it in front of you, you can come against the attacks of the enemy that tries to come and steal your word from your heart.

We have to fearlessly confront the demonic forces that come against us. We have to be bold, courageous, and stand in the authority and power God has given us.

Know that God's spoken words have a creative power about them. God can even create what is necessary to cause them to come to pass, especially when we believe them and actually speak them out loud, with faith. We are actually repeating, here on Earth, what God has spoken to us from Heaven.

Mark 11:23 For assuredly, I say to you, whoever says to this mountain, 'Be removed and be cast into the sea,' and does not doubt in his heart, but believes that those things he says will be done, he will have whatever he says.

It is also very important not to add to your prophetic words. Also, remember that we do not always interpret our prophetic words correctly. Our interpretations can be wrong, whereas God's word is not. If we obey, and cooperate with God's words, in due time, it will be accomplished, if we do not quit.

It is so important to respect God. Know that as a prophet there is great responsibility. We always have to be faithful to speak what God has given us and at the time He tells us to give it.

CHAPTER 12 God uses prophecy to transfer His word to the people

Many people want to make prophecy something that is hard. They feel that everyone cannot prophecy. Prophesying is simply speaking what God gives you by the Holy Spirit. It is God's desire that we all prophecy. We should not be afraid to step out and prophecy. People say all the time I am afraid that I will say the wrong thing. I am afraid that I will not speak from God but speak from my own self.

I tell them as long as you are building that person up even if it is you, you have not done any harm. You still blessed that person. We all have to learn, and we all have to practice.

When you first start out prophesying over people it is all about lifting them up. We do not need to prophecy regarding them selling their home, getting married, divorcing, changing jobs, or anything that could really hurt them if you are wrong. We need to leave this type of prophecy to a more seasoned prophet.

Trust God that you are able to hear His voice clearly and know what He is saying. Then immediately say and do what He has told you to do.

All believers can be trained and activated to flow in the gift of prophecy. This is because all believers have the Holy Spirit, and the Holy Spirit has all the gifts, including prophecy. Therefore, all believers have this in them also because the Holy Spirit is in them.

John 10:27 says: "My sheep hear My voice, and I know them, and they follow Me."

The gift of prophecy is just speaking under the inspiration of God to bring edification, exhortation, and comfort to people.

Corinthians 14:3 tells us this, it says, but the one who prophesies speaks to people for their strengthening, encouraging and comfort.

The more we prophecy the better we will become. For example, if a musician does not practice, he will not get any better.

Prophesying is the same way, the more we practice the better and more comfortable we become.

When I first came to Vision Church Christian International, I was put on the prophetic team during a major conference. The lady I was with had been at the church for a very long time. I stood there and listened to her as she prophesied over people. She was a nabi prophet like me. I was amazed at how well she flowed. Just listening to her was just a beautiful sound in my ear. After we finished, I asked her how did she learned to prophecy like that? She said practice and she was so right.

I work at Christian International as the Vision Investment Partner Director. One of my jobs is to prophecy over all the Vision Investment Partners. I am also on the prophetic team and we prophecy on Friday nights. So, I get a lot of practice and I love it. It keeps me ready and equipped at all times.

I have three sisters and when they come down to Florida to visit me, they love being a part of the ministry and they hate to go home. They always say we get so filled up and then we get dry because we have no one to minister to. I tell them prophecy over people on television. Prophecy over their families. I used to ask God on Wednesday and Sunday's what the pastor was going to preach about. It would really build my faith when I would get to church, and the pastor would preach what God had told me. This really increased my faith level.

God still tells me things just to let me know I am hearing Him.

At our 2022 Christmas gathering, my children gave me a blanket with all their dogs pictures on it. They have a total of nine dogs. I call them my grand dogs. They are all very special to me. But before they gave me the blanket God told me I was going to receive it.

That same Christmas, the day after Christmas I always go to the store and buy my grandkid's Christmas ornaments for the next year since they are half price. God told me my son's wife was pregnant, and for me to buy and extra ornament. Later that week my son told me they were expecting.

Another time God told me my sons were going to buy me an I-phone watch. When it arrived, it was in a box and my husband handed me the box and said this is for you from the boys. I said it is an I-phone watch and it was. I just love it when God does that.

When my youngest daughter was pregnant with her second child, she said oh mama I know it is a girl. But when she told me she was pregnant the words immediately came out of my mouth, a prophet of the Lord. So, I knew it was a boy, but I did not tell her. But he was a boy.

I believe God does this for me, because He wants me to always know that He is speaking to me, and that I am hearing Him. He wants me to keep my faith level up and I love it.

When God speaks to us, it is normally in a still small voice that we hear. It flows in a continuous flow. It is not a loud voice. It is peaceful and calm. It can easily be overlooked if you choose to ignore it and do not pay attention.

You do not have to be a lawyer, doctor, or highly educated to prophecy. God looks at our heart not our education. You can be poor, rich, or in between it does not matter. God wants us to be bold, and not be afraid to step out and give others what God gives us to give them.

Do not stop and analyze or try to understand what you are giving someone. Just speak out what you hear. The enemy wants us to doubt what we hear from God. When we doubt that it is from God, it keeps us from hearing God's voice clearly. It is like being in a telephone conversation with someone you know well, and

continually asking that person if that is
really them.

God wants us to be courageous. Allow
Him to move us to a place with Him that
in the natural, we would not be
comfortable. But trusting Him, we can and
will be comfortable.

See yourself as an overcomer, one that has
great faith, one that will dare to step out
even if it seems uncomfortable to you.

Become radical before the Lord. Arise in
the plans He has for you. Do not doubt,
keep pushing forward. Press through even
if sometimes it may seem uncomfortable.
God wants us to know that His glory
anointing will increase in us as we step out
and push ourselves.

God wants us to enter into His gates with
praise and worship in our heart. Know that
as we enter in, He is there with us. We will
be in His presence and where the presence
of the Lord is there is great freedom.

In the Old Testament prophetic ministry seemed to be used to give guidance, direction, and counsel etc. to God's people. Prophetic ministry is used now for all the above.

The gift of prophecy is specifically mentioned in 1 Corinthians 12:10 and Ephesians 4:11.

1 Corinthians 12:10 it says, to another the working of miracles, to another prophecy, to another discerning of spirits, to another different kinds of tongues, to another the interpretation of tongues.

Ephesians 4:11 says, And He Himself gave some to be apostles, some prophets, some evangelists, and some pastors and teachers.

CHAPTER 13 Keys of a prophet

Prophetic words are given to us to build up the church, to know the mind and will of Christ for our lives as believers.

Acts 2:17 tells us that your sons and daughters will prophecy and your young men shall see visons, and your old men shall dream dreams.

A prophet receives revelations and directions from the Lord for our benefit. A prophet can see into the future and tell us things that will keep us from making the wrong decisions, or to warn us about something that is coming. God communicates to His church through His prophets.

A prophet is called by God to be one of His representatives on earth. When a prophet speaks, it is as if God is speaking. So, it is so important to not add anything to what God is giving you, as you give the word to someone. It is not our place to interpret the prophetic word we give.

If you give a prophetic word to someone, and they say I do not understand what you are talking about. Tell them that you are just the messenger God is flowing through. Tell them to write the prophetic word out, then they need to pray over it. Have them take it to their leader or overseer to help understand it. Sometimes when you get a prophetic word and you do not understand it, it is not time for it to be revealed to you. I tell people when this happens to put it on a shelf and wait, if it is God it will come to pass.

Know that God is neither male nor female. If you are doing an activation (a training exercise), where you are having to give a prophetic word without knowing if they are male or female, do not be concerned if you say my daughter and you are prophesying over a male or vice versa.

One time I was in an activation, and it was called the blindman activation. In this activation you did not know the person who was behind you. You just had to step out and prophecy. I began to prophecy over this person, and I started out my daughter. I prophesied over her for a while then God said my son. I was really confused. But I obeyed God and said my son and begin to prophecy. When we finished the activation and turned around there was a tiny lady in front of me.

I told the instructor what had happened. He knew the young lady, and he told me she is a single mom, and she has to be both mom and dad to her children. In the natural I would have thought I had missed God, but I did not miss Him. I was so glad I obeyed God and stepped out of my comfort zone and allowed God to stretch me.

Another time before I realized God did not see male or female, we were doing that same activation. I was standing behind this lady and she began to prophecy over me. When she began to prophecy over me, she said my son. When she said my son, I shut down and I did not listen to anything she had said. I thought she had missed it because she called me a son. When we finished the activation and went back to our seats, someone asked the instructor what if you were a female and they addressed you as a male when they prophesied over you.

The instructor said, God does not see male or female, so the word would still be accurate. I was so disappointed because I did not listen to the word that was prophesied over me. I learned something that day, and from then on, I did not care if they called me male or female. I still listened and received the word that they were giving me.

CHAPTER 14 Summary

In summary, if you are a Christian, you have the Holy Spirit and through the Holy Spirit, you too can hear and sense God communicating to you. You too can prophesy!

God wants you to hear Him. He wants you to recognize Him communicating with you. It may be by hearing a still small voice in your spirit. It may be by getting a short flash of a picture or vision, or it may be by you just sensing something in your spirit.

Pay attention to these "proddings" by the Holy Spirit, and they will become a blessing both to you and to others. They will also become a guide and a warning to help you and lead you in your everyday life.

Fay Velez

Contact Information

Contact us through the contact form on our website:

thomasvelez.com

To order more books by Fay Velez:
- The Power of Prayer that brings Healings & Miracles
- Spirits that Keep us Bound
- Powerful Nuggets from the Lord
- Going from Ungodly to Godly
- Spirits that try to stay Hidden
- Hearing the Voice of God Daily
- Spirits that Destroy Churches & Businesses
- Unlocking the Prophetic in us
- Get Free Stay Free (Thomas & Fay Velez)

To order more books by Thomas Velez:
- Personal Spiritual Warfare
- Army of the Lord Arising
- Understanding the Book of Revelation
- Antichrist Invades the Earth

- God saved My Life 29 Times

Order books online from websites:

thomasvelez.com

and also at:

Amazon.com

Made in the USA
Columbia, SC
31 May 2024

36465709R00043